BEYOND THE CROSS
Sanctification
A Lost Teaching of the Church

BEYOND THE CROSS
Sanctification
A Lost Teaching of the Church

Pamela Jackson

AGAPE
Publishing, Inc.

PUBLISHED BY AGAPE PUBLISHING, INC.
12600 Deerfield Parkway, Ste. 125, Alpharetta, GA 30004
United States of America
678-684-1500

ISBN: 978-0-6151-6449-6
Library of Congress Control Number: 2007907259

©2007 Pamela Jackson
All rights reserved, which includes the right to reproduce
this book or portions thereof in any form whatsoever except
as provided by the U.S. Copyright Law.

Printed in the United States of America

In memory of my great-great-great uncle, Sam Keen.

*For Suzy Hill,
who unknowingly has been an inspiration to me.*

When we come to the foot of the Cross and look toward Jesus, it is glorious. But, if we do not spiritually move beyond the Cross, then we are living in the shadow of Jesus' death and not the fullness of His life.

-Pamela Jackson

Acknowledgements

FOREMOST, I ACKNOWLEDGE that it is by the grace of God that I have written this book. For without Him, I am nothing.

This entire work has been created due to my great-great-great uncle, Sam Keen, who was a well-known Methodist minister in the late 1800's. This book is based on his work on sanctification. Parts of this book include verbatim work of his which is now part of the public domain.

I am so thankful for my grandmother, the late Juliette Gwendolyn Sparks McClellan, for being my spiritual guide, for teaching me about God, showing me how to pray, and being a constant mirror who reflected the Light. I am so grateful to her for entrusting to me the writings of Uncle Sam.

I owe much to Reverend Joe Bowen and Reverend Malone Dodson, both United Methodist ministers and true servants of God, who so graciously imparted to me their knowledge. I thank you for all of your support, generosity, and love.

My heart belongs to my children Juliette, Jeffrey, Cameron, and Annaleigh –you are each the light of my life. I hope that you will find use for this book in your own lives. I thank my mother, Caroline Allen, who helped me to come this far as a writer by always encouraging my writing as a young girl and even now, as I age. I am also blessed to have so many who are always there for me, especially Daddy, Jo, my dearest and best friend Denise Jacob, and my spiritual mentor Judi Collins. Thank you so much for everything.

There are no words sufficient for my deep gratitude for my husband, Dale. The power of the Living God has been more evident in you than I have ever witnessed elsewhere. Lightning does not strike in the same place twice; then again, God does not need second chances. I love you.

Table of Contents

Introduction xiii

Chapter 1   *The Forms of Sanctification* 1

Chapter 2   *The Accessories and Agencies* 11

Chapter 3   *The Essentiality* 19

Chapter 4   *The Elements* 22

Chapter 5   *The Advantages* 26

Chapter 6   *Attainability* 29

Chapter 7   *Liberty* 32

Chapter 8   *The Bondage of Sin* 36

Chapter 9   *On Becoming a Servant of God* 41

Chapter 10 *Reasonable Believing* 44

Introduction

STEP INSIDE THE doors of any church and ask the first ten people you see if they have heard the word *sanctification*. The majority of those people will say, "No." Now, ask the few who have heard the word *sanctification* to define it. The likelihood is that few can. If, by chance, there is someone among the group who can define *sanctification,* the probability is they really do not understand it. *Sanctification* is one of the basic elements at the very core of Christianity, yet, at some point in history it has become a rarely understood term.

Hebrews 12:14 (NAS) reads: "Pursue peace with all men, and the sanctification without which no one will see the Lord." It is most important to notice the article "the" placed in front of the word *sanctification* in this Scripture; it helps us to understand that there is a *sanctification* that is "the" *sanctification*, which must be distinguished from other forms of *sanctification*. The Bible teaches us that there are various forms of *sanctification*. However, there is one form that is *"the"* sanctification. For the purposes of this book, it will be called *sanctification "par excellence"* and it is distinct from all other modes of *sanctification. The sanctification "par excellence"* is specifically *the sanctification* of *the Holy Spirit.*

Before any of this begins to make sense we must first define and understand the word *sanctification*. S*anctification* is a noun meaning: the act or process of sanctifying or the state of being sanctified (Webster). Stemming from the word sanctify, which is a verb and means to make holy; render sacred or morally or spiritually pure; cleansed from sin; to set apart as holy (Webster). For example: The

Sabbath was sanctified by God. More fully the definition of *sanctification* is the gracious work of the Holy Spirit whereby the believer is freed from sin and exalted to holiness of heart and life.

At the risk of seeming tedious, here is a list of a few other words stemming from the word sanctify as define by Webster:

> *Sanctificationist* –noun, one who has become sanctified
>
> *Sanctifier* –noun, one who or that which sanctifies: The Holy Spirit
>
> *Sanction* –verb, to approve authoritatively; solemn and final confirmation by supreme authority
>
> *Sanctuary* –noun, a holy or sacred place
>
> *Sanctimony* –noun, affected or hypocritical devoutness or saintliness
>
> *Sanctimonious* –adjective, making an ostentatious display or a hypocritical pretense of sanctity; affecting holiness or piety

The very word *sanctification*, which is the process of becoming holy, is a very fundamental basis of Christianity. But, before looking further into *the sanctification "par excellence"* which is given pre-eminence over all forms of *sanctification*, we need to understand the other forms of *sanctification* which Scripture, indeed, teaches.

Chapter 1

THE FORMS OF SANCTIFICATION

I. Provisional Sanctification

> *"Now crowned with glory and honor because He [Jesus] suffered death, so that by the grace of God He [Jesus] might taste death for everyone." (Hebrews 2:9 NIV)*

> *"For by one offering He has perfected for all time those who are sanctified." (Hebrews 10:14 NAS)*

CHRIST, BY THE sacrifice of Himself through his death and sufferings as atonement for all sin, brought the whole human race into a sanctified relationship with God. This is provisional sanctification. In such, through Jesus' death on the Cross, I believe God looks upon all souls as hallowed unto Himself. This is very important to understand. Every living soul has been sprinkled by the blood of Jesus. EVERYONE. Look back at Hebrews 2:9, it clearly says, "everyone". The word "everyone" is very clearly understood to include all people, which means all "bad" people as well as all "good" people. It means every Jew, every Muslim, every Christian, every Buddhist, every Hindu –EVERYONE! Everyone is sanctified to God because of the blood of Jesus.

This is the most basic form of sanctification and it is obvious that a large part of this world does not understand it –even among Christians. Our lack of understanding is most evident in our religious warfare against each other. We are arrogant in our thinking that God loves people of one faith more than the people of another. Personally, I believe that one group may grieve God more than another, but *love*, no. We exemplify our belief of God's partiality by fighting to the death to prove our point. Please, do not confuse that statement with a need to defend ourselves or our country. But, at some point in history we all have been guilty of killing to prove a point about whose God He really is. If you do not believe that statement, just look at the Cross.

Provisional sanctification, which occurred by the sacrifice of Jesus, is a constructive sanctification under the plan of redemption. And, it cannot be more clearly understood. "Everyone" is sanctified to God. It is real and it is fundamental, but it is not *the sanctification "par excellence"*.

THINK ABOUT IT…

1. ***Do you believe that Jesus died on the Cross for everyone?***

2. ***For whom do you believe Jesus died?***

3. ***In your own words describe your understanding of Hebrews 2:9.***

II. Partial Sanctification

WHEN WE MAKE the conscious decision to turn toward Christ, this is when an actual "work" of *sanctification* is begun. Partial sanctification is when the human soul begins to take action. When a person chooses to accept Christ, regeneration begins to take shape. Not only is a new life imparted, but a new nature is given to the soul. It is at this point that *the Spirit* is in germinal form and the graces of *the Spirit*: love, joy, peace, patience, goodness, kindness, and faithfulness are implanted with the new birth of the person who has consciously turned toward Christ. It is now that a "work" of *sanctification*, true and deep, is wrought in the soul. Still, this is not the sanctification *"par excellence"*.

THINK ABOUT IT…

1. *Have you turned toward Christ?*

2. *Do you feel that the graces of the Spirit are evident in yourself?*

3. *Can you recognize the graces of the Spirit in others?*

III. Personal Sanctification

WITH PARTIAL SANCTIFICATION a new life is now begotten in the soul of the believer. This new life comes with an instinctive impulse to give oneself into Christian service. In doing so, we become personally sanctified to God in Christian work. This is personal sanctification. For instance, I knew a man who was a very talented and successful physician. That success allowed him many privileges of a financial nature, with which there is nothing wrong. But, he was very self-serving and careless of others' feelings and needs. In general, he was a heathen. One day something happened in his life which turned him toward Christ, and a new life and new nature began in him. With this new life he felt the need to serve God with the gifts of his profession. He began doing medical missionary work in third world countries. Now, for the last ten years he has been a self-sacrificing toiler for God. This is his *personal sanctification* to God in work.

On a more at home level, many people who were not raised in the church come to church for the first time because they are at a crisis point in their life and they are seeking comfort, and indeed, the Body of Christ is a glorious place to find comfort. At this point of crisis many people turn to Christ for the first time. In this revelation of a newly imparted life there is the natural impulse to serve God through the church. So we begin to sign up –Sunday School teacher, nursery worker, altar guild, usher –the list could be endless. This is *personal sanctification* to this blessed work for God.

Frances Ridley Havergal wrote the beautiful hymn, *Take My Life, and Let It Be*. The words so beautifully exemplify this desire for personal sanctification.

> *Take my life, and let it be*
> *Consecrated, Lord, to thee.*
> *Take my moments and my days;*
> *Let them flow in ceaseless praise.*
> *Take my hands, and let them move*
> *At the impulse of thy love.*
> *Take my feet, and let them be*
> *Swift and beautiful for thee.*

This hymn voices the gracious impulses of the soul with a new life begotten and its desire to be sanctified to service as a personal sacrifice to God.

> *As a side note I would like to say that even in light of the trend toward contemporary music, I am an advocate of continuing the use of the hymnal in church services, even if combined with contemporary music. Here is why –the hymnal is rich with theology and has been a source of not only comfort through the ages, but of valuable, ageless lessons. I fear that we are at risk of raising a generation of children and youth who will have no idea what a hymnal is. That would be a tragedy.*

This personal sanctification is glorious, but it is still not *the sanctification "par excellence"*. It is also important to point out that it is entirely possible for one to be wholly consecrated to Christian service without having *the sanctification of the Spirit*.

A preacher friend of mine told a story about a man who had been a member of his congregation for nearly twenty years. The man never missed a day of church; he served on several committees, and graciously volunteered anytime there was a need. He was a pillar of the church. My preacher friend said that at one particular service when he offered an altar call for anyone who was ready to accept Jesus in their life, he was astonished when this gentleman came forward. My preacher friend said he kneeled beside him and the gentleman said to him that although he had spent most of his life serving God he realized he had never accepted Jesus into his heart.

The gentleman, of whom my preacher friend was speaking, was certainly a servant of God and was sanctified to God in his work, but he was not sanctified to God in his soul. There are so many people just like this who, in a like manner, are wholly devoted to serving God and are wholly consecrated to Christian work, yet they have complete unrest in their soul. Why? They are personally sanctified to God in service, but are not sanctified of the Spirit in their hearts. Many of these people are vainly hoping that if they multiply their self-sacrifice and toil, they will receive inward deliverance and come to a state of rest and enjoyment in God because of their own outward actions. Hence, if you are using the concept of "work, work, work" as the way to reach a real and meaningful relationship with God, while well intended and good, you are defeating yourself. You are merely deferring your hope of *the sanctification "par excellence"* and the heart remains empty. In general, we tend to ignore this emptiness until the heart becomes faint or sick. Oftentimes, it is not until a person is faced with the reality of death that they seek complete sanctification.

I am not a huge fan of country music, but I am largely impressed at the depth of the understanding of life which country music writers tend to possess. There is one song in particular I find exceptionally deep. It is a song by Tim Nichols and Craig Wiseman sung by country artist Tim McGraw called, *Live like You Were Dying*. The theme of this song is about a man who finds out that he has a terminal disease. He consults with a friend that had previously been given a similar diagnosis, looking for advice on how to cope with news of this kind. This is what his friend said he did when he learned he was dying:

> *I went sky diving,*
> *I went Rocky Mountain climbing,*
> *I went 2.7 seconds on a bull name Fu Man Chu.*
> *And I loved deeper and I spoke sweeter,*
> *And I gave forgiveness I'd been denying.*
> *I was finally the husband,*
> *That most the time I wasn't.*
> *And I became a friend a friend would like to have.*
> *And all of a sudden goin' fishin'*
> *Wasn't such an imposition,*
> *And I went three times that year I lost my Dad.*
> *Well, I finally read the Good Book,*
> *And I took a good long hard look,*
> *At what I'd do if I could do it all again.*
> *And some day I hope you get the chance*
> *To live like you were dying.*

Beyond the Cross

Why is it that we have a tendency to wait until somebody tells us that we are going to die before we really start to live and do the things we should have been doing all along? Let me break the news to you – we are all dying. Each and every one of us suffers a fatal disease. It is called birth. Birth is a terminal condition.

THINK ABOUT IT...

1. *Do you have a desire to serve God? Why?*

2. *Do you volunteer at your church? What volunteer jobs are you doing?*

3. *Do you have unrest in your soul?*

4. *Do you believe that your service to God will deliver you from unrest?*

5. *Do you work for God as a means to become closer to Him?*

IV. Preparatory Sanctification

"Cleanse your hands, you sinners, and purify your hearts." (James 4:8 NAS)

"Sanctify Christ as Lord in your hearts." (1 Peter 3:15 NAS)

*"For I **am** the L*ORD *your God: ye shall therefore sanctify yourselves, and ye shall be holy." (Leviticus 11:44 KJ)*

"Cleanse our consciences from acts that lead to death, so that we may serve the living God!" (Hebrews 9:14 NIV)

EXHORTATIONS SUCH AS "sanctify yourselves" and "cleanse yourselves" recur throughout Scripture. These sorts of statements are telling us to put ourselves into such an attitude, as God has commanded, in order that He may wholly sanctify us. We cannot cleanse ourselves or make ourselves holy. None of us has the power to sanctify ourselves to God. But, through the atonement and by the grace that has already been given, we do have the ability to commit ourselves to God. We have the ability to trust the promises of God, so that God, the Holy Spirit, can cleanse and sanctify us wholly.

Suppose your body has an infection and you are very sick. Someone could come to you and say, "Heal yourself!" Our reply would certainly be, "I would, if I could!" But, we do not have the ability to heal ourselves just like that. However, we do have the ability to pick up the telephone, make a doctor's appointment, and commit ourselves to going. The doctor will give us an antibiotic and we can commit to taking it. And when we do, we are restored. In the same manner there is *preparatory sanctification* –a giving of the soul up to God to be restored and made whole.

Provisional, partial, personal, and preparatory *sanctification* are all blessed, invaluable, and Biblical forms of *sanctification*, but they are not *the sanctification "par excellence"* or *the sanctification of the Spirit*. It is *the sanctification of the Spirit* which cleanses the heart of all sin and fills the heart with all the fullness of God. This *sanctification* is Pentecostal in its power because the Holy Spirit is the source and only the Holy Spirit can accomplish this *sanctification*.

THINK ABOUT IT...

    1. Have you committed yourself to God?

    2. Are you in such a state that The Holy Spirit can cleanse you of your inward sin?

V. The Sanctification "Par Excellence"

THE DISTINGUISHING CHARACTERISTIC of *the sanctification of the Spirit*, as suggested in the name itself is that it is "of the Spirit." It is finally the Holy Spirit that cleanses us, and no other intervening accessory or agency. It is the Holy Spirit that completes *the sanctification*. But, it is first mandatory that we, the human agency, prepare ourselves to receive the Holy Spirit.

> ***"Present your bodies a living and holy sacrifice, acceptable to God." (Romans 12:1 NAS)***

We must choose to turn away from sin of the flesh and spirit and the filthiness of the world at large. For it is only in this attitude that *the sanctification of the Spirit* can become operative in the soul.

Our personal decision to be separated from sin and consecrated wholly to God is only the condition for *the sanctification of the Spirit*, but it is not the source of *the sanctification of the Spirit*. We, as the human agency, stand at the beginning of the process of the *sanctification of the Spirit*, but it is the agency of the Holy Spirit that consummates it, thus receiving *the sanctification "par excellence"*.

THINK ABOUT IT...

> *1. Have you prepared yourself to respond to the leadings of the Holy Spirit?*

> *2. Have you conscientiously chosen to turn away from sin?*

Chapter 2

THE ACCESSORIES AND AGENCIES

I BRIEFLY MENTIONED accessories and agencies in the previous chapter and would like to more fully explain, as I feel that this understanding helps greatly in understanding The Trinity, as well as *the sanctification of the Spirit*.

The process of *the sanctification of the Spirit* may, at first glance, seem to be attributed to two different classes: accessories and agencies. It would seem that the process is sometimes effected by one and sometimes effected by the other. But, comprehensive study of The Scriptures shows us that *the sanctification of the Spirit* is a resultant process of the combination of the accessories and agencies together. One is instrumental, the other efficient; one is the prophet's staff, the other the prophet's power. That is to say that one is only effective as conjoined to the presence of the other. *The sanctification of the Spirit* is *through* one, but *by* the other.

THE ACCESSORIES

1. THE BLOOD

In all stages of *sanctification* –provisional, partial, personal, preparatory, and *the sanctification "par excellence"* —it is ascribed to the blood.

> *"In Him we have redemption through His blood." (Ephesians 1:7 NAS)*
>
> *"God presented Him as a sacrifice of atonement, through faith in his blood." (Romans 3:25 NIV)*
>
> *"They have washed their robes and made them white in the blood of the Lamb." (Revelation 7:14 NIV)*

The blood of Jesus bears a very intimate relation to the cleansing of the soul. But, we must understand that in the process of *the sanctification of the Spirit*, the function of the blood is not effectual, but rather provisional. That is, the blood does not bring about *the sanctification of the Spirit*, but it does provide the basis for it. The blood is the condition upon which the Holy Spirit can accomplish the cleansing of the soul. The blood is the provision by which the sanctifying agent, the Holy Spirit, can come in contact with the soul in order that it may cleanse it. The blood avails when accepted by faith that it is the divine provision for *the sanctification of the Spirit*. It is the blood that secures *the* sanctifying power of *the Spirit* through faith. When the blood is accepted by faith, then the Spirit responds and the work of *the sanctification of the Spirit* has begun. Hence, but if not for the blood as the provision for our redemption, the Holy Spirit could not renew, cleanse, fill, and empower the soul. The blood is a cleansing *accessory*, but not a cleansing *agent*.

2. THE TRUTH

The truth in the process of *the sanctification of the Spirit* is very prominent in Scripture.

> *"Sanctify them by the truth." (John 17:17 NIV)*
>
> *"But whoever lives by the truth comes into the light." (John 3:21 NIV)*

The preposition "by" associated with the word "truth" tells us a great deal –*by the truth*. It tells us that truth is a channel of sanctification, and not a source. The truth (Scripture) is that which conveys the sanctifying power, but it does not possess a sanctifying energy in itself. The truth is important in the process of *the sanctification of the Spirit* because it reveals the need for cleansing, the privilege of cleansing, and the method by which the cleansing takes place. The truth is impotent to do the work of cleansing, but it is powerful in bringing the soul to the source of cleansing. *The sanctification of the Spirit* does not come without the truth, but neither does *the sanctification of the Spirit* come by the truth. It is the promise of cleansing, but not the power for cleansing. The truth tells us of the grace of cleansing. If the soul accepts the magnificent offer we are given in the truth, then the Spirit responds and the process of *the sanctification of the Spirit* continues. Hence, the truth is the appointed *accessory* for the attainment, maintenance, and development of holiness in experience and life.

3. Faith

It is a Scriptural truth that sanctification is by faith.

> ***"Your faith has saved you, go in peace." (Luke 7:50 NIV)***

> ***"He purified their hearts by faith." (Acts 15:9 NIV)***

> ***"So that they may receive forgiveness of sins and a place among those who are sanctified by faith in me." (Acts 26:18 NIV)***

Faith is the means by which the blood and the truth become available to *the sanctification of the Spirit*. Faith accepts the blood as the ground, the truth as the channel, and the Spirit as the source of cleansing (see Diagram 1). Calling them agencies and accessories helps clarify this very complicated schematic. You see, faith is not the sanctifying agent, but it is the sanctifying instrument. Faith does the work of sanctification instrumentally, but not actually. It is faith in the truth of the promise, which the blood brought for the cleansing of the soul, by the power of the Holy Spirit, which brings about *the sanctification of the Spirit*. Therefore, any attempt to secure *the sanctification of the Spirit* other than by faith is a failure and contrary to the methods of grace.

> ***"Therefore, the promise comes by faith." (Romans 4:16 NIV)***

Hence, many people are left confused as to why they have still not come to peace and inward cleansing when the have spent numerous hours, days, and years toiling in Christian service, repeated consecrations, and shedding of many tears. The explanation is that they have, under a misapprehension, sought *the sanctification of the Spirit* by their Christian service, consecrations, and tears, when it was by faith and only faith that *the sanctification of the Spirit* could be sought. It is faith that accepts the blood in its purifying efficiency, and relies upon the promises of the truth in the grace of *the sanctification of the Spirit*. And, God says to the seeking soul, "According to your faith will it be done to you." (Matthew 9:29). The wonderful hymn, *My Faith Looks Up to Thee*, expresses how our soul answers back. The words read like this:

> *My faith looks up to thee,*
> *Thou Lamb of Calvary, Savior divine!*
> *Now hear me while I pray,*
> *Take all my guilt away.*
> *O let me from this day,*
> *Be wholly thine!*

As we have seen, the accessories are the blood, the truth, and faith. However, with all the importance that the accessories hold, they would be valueless without the agencies.

Diagram 1

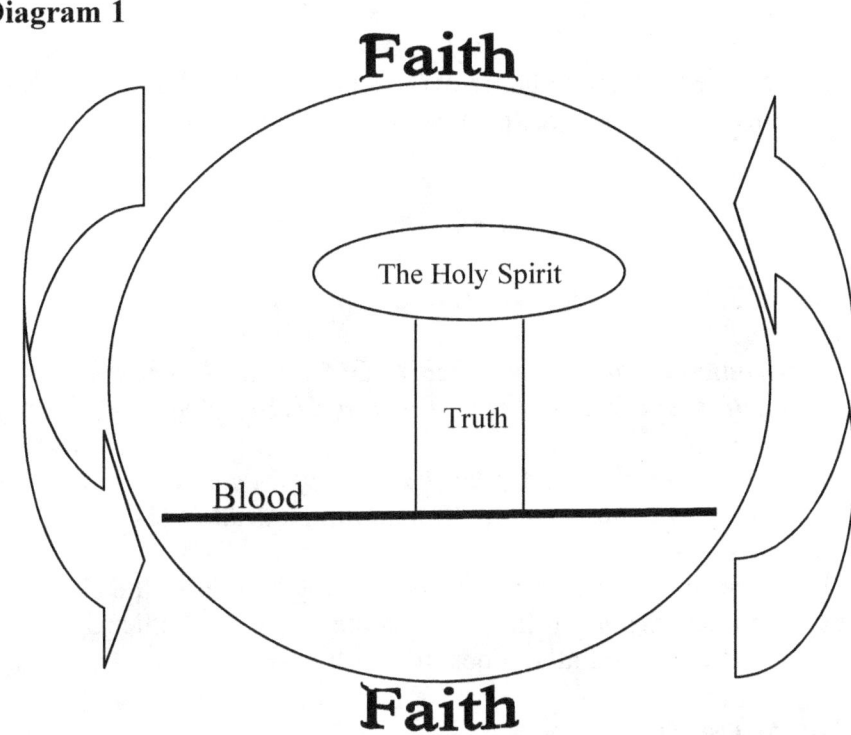

1. *The Holy Spirit is the source of the cleansing which we are seeking. It is the Holy Spirit that accomplishes the cleansing within us. (The sanctification of the Spirit)*
2. *The blood is the ground. It was Jesus' death for our sins that allows the Holy Spirit to accomplish the cleansing of our souls.*
3. *The Truth (Scripture) tells us of our need for cleansing, tells us of the privilege of cleansing, tells us of the method by which the cleansing takes place. The Truth is the promise.*
4. *Faith encircles the entire process. We must have faith that the blood is the grounds for cleansing, the truth is the channel for cleansing, and the Holy Spirit is the source of the cleansing.*

THE AGENCIES

The agencies are every being of The Trinity. The Father, the Son, and the Holy Spirit –all three have very specific functions, yet they are one.

1. THE AGENCY OF THE FATHER

It is the Father that sends the Spirit.

> *"Create in me a clean heart, O God, and renew a steadfast spirit within me." (Psalms 51:10 NAS)*

> *"Now may the God [the Father] of peace Himself sanctify you entirely." (I Thessalonians 5:23 NAS)*

The Father grants the prayer of the seeking soul after the cleansing through the intercession of the Son. It is the act of the Father by which we are sanctified. The Father does the work *authoritatively*.

2. THE AGENCY OF THE SON

It is the blood of the Son that has brought the gift of the Holy Spirit.

> *"Jesus, that He might sanctify the people through His own blood, suffered outside the gate." (Hebrews 13:12 NAS)*

> *"God presented Him as a sacrifice of atonement, through faith in His blood." (Romans 3:25 NIV)*

The Son stood in the presence of God for us. He took our sins upon Himself and gave His blood so that we may be cleansed and be available to receive the promised gift of the Holy Spirit. It is the act of the Son by which we are sanctified. The Son does the work *mediatorially*.

3. THE AGENCY OF THE HOLY SPIRIT

This grace is distinctively called *the sanctification of the Spirit*. It is the Holy Spirit that effectuates *the sanctification*. The Holy Spirit accompanies and energizes all the accessories. The Holy Spirit executes the will of the Father and the desire of the Son. It is the act of the Holy Spirit by which we are sanctified. The Holy Spirit does the work *administratively*.

> *The Father grants the cleansing, the Son dispenses the cleansing, and the Holy Spirit imparts the cleansing.*

The hymn, *O Come and Dwell in Me*, so beautifully expresses the depth of the soul filled with the Holy Spirit. The words read:

> *O come and dwell in me,*
> *Spirit of power within,*
> *And bring the glorious liberty*
> *From sorrow, fear, and sin.*
> *Hasten the joyful day,*
> *Which shall my sins consume,*
> *When old thing shall be done away,*
> *And all things new become.*

 THINK ABOUT IT…

1. *What are the three accessories to the sanctification of the Spirit?*

2. *What are the three agencies?*

3. *What does the Truth (Scripture) provide us?*

4. *How is faith the key element?*

Chapter 3

THE ESSENTIALITY

WE HAVE BEEN graciously offered the gift of eternal life. No if, ands, or buts. It is there and is ours for the taking. But it is essential that we prepare ourselves for such a gift.

> *"Pursue peace with all men, and the sanctification without which no one will see the Lord." (Hebrews 12:14 NAS)*

Many Christians dislike the book of Revelation. It is a hard book to understand and it is simply hard to fathom. But, how beautifully the idea of the essentiality of *the sanctification of the Spirit* is relayed to us in Revelation 7:13. John tells the story like this:

> *"Then one of the elders asked me, 'These in white robes –who are they, and where did they come from?' I answered, 'Sir, you know.' And he said, 'These are they who have come out of great tribulation; they have washed their robes and made them white in the blood of the Lamb.' Therefore, 'they are before the throne of God and serve him day and night in his temple; and he who sits on the throne will spread his tent over them. Never again will they hunger; never again will they thirst. The sun will not beat upon them, nor any scorching heat. For the Lamb at the center of the*

> *throne will be their shepherd; he will lead them to springs of living water. And God will wipe away every tear from their eyes.'" NIV*

Those that stood there were all white-robed; all were blood-washed. Simply stated what this passage relays to us is that we must prepare ourselves so that we may join the "sacred throng."

I knew a teenage girl who had a friend that had been in a severe car accident. He was not expected to live and, in fact, he did not. He was in a coma for three days before he finally passed away. The teenage girl was terribly distraught because she did not believe that he had given his life to Christ (been saved). She was upset because now that he was in a coma she could not talk with him and tell him about Christ. She was afraid that he would not have eternal life. This is what I said to her, "Why do you limit God to your own ability? You may not be able to communicate with your friend because he is in a coma, but do you believe that stops God?"

God had three days, in our timeframe, to be alone with this boy before he passed. I whole-heartedly believe that God loved this child far more than any being on this earth could possibly have loved him. I believe that God, more than anyone, wanted this boy to have eternal life. And, I have to believe that God reconciled this boy to Himself before his final passing. I have to believe this because I have faith in the promise that God loves all His children. I believe the blood of Jesus can even be effectual in the transition of death and can cleanse the desiring soul. I believe the Holy Spirit had the ability to sanctify this boy and his soul was fitted in a white robe that had been blood washed.

As Christians, we have heard the call; we have seen the Light. But, for all practical purposes we skate along the edge of holiness. We are unwilling to make the consecration, or to enter into the struggle against the secular world at large. We neglect, sometimes reject, and not infrequently despise the conditions of such a life. So we live, so we die. Is it any wonder that so many professing Christians come to the hour of death and are unprepared and afraid to die? A great many people, when knowingly have reached the last days of life, are consumed with a feeling of, "If I just had more time to pray," or "I need time to get some matters fixed between God and me." Why do we wait? Why do we choose not to wear the white robes of holiness today? The white robes of holiness are not exclusive to any group and they are not intended simply for church events. They are everyday wear. We can walk the earth in them, be at home in them, be on the streets in them, work in them, and shop in them.

My grandmother was a wonderful Christian lady. When it became evident that her days in this life were coming to an end, I asked her, "Are you prepared?" She replied, "I have nothing left to do." Her praying was finished, her garments were washed –she was ready. She had nothing to do. I would think that dying would be more than enough to have on ones hands without having anything else to deal with when death comes. Unfortunately, so many of us have so much to do and do not realize that we have so little time in which to do it. How wonderful it would be that when death comes we could say, "I have nothing to do!"

THINK ABOUT IT...

1. ***Why is it essential that we prepare ourselves to receive the gift of the Holy Spirit?***

2. ***If you learned today that you were soon to die, would you be spiritually prepared?***

3. ***If you were facing death, what about your life would you change?***

Chapter 4

THE ELEMENTS

THERE IS REST in the soul which is particular to the personal indwelling of the Spirit.

> *"Come to me, all you who are weary and burdened, and I will give you rest." (Matthew 11:28 NIV)*
>
> *"Take my yoke upon you and learn from me, for I am gentle and humble in heart, and you will find rest for your souls." (Matthew 11:29 NIV)*
>
> *"This then is how we know that we belong to the truth, and how we set our hearts at rest in His presence." (1 John 3:19 NIV)*

The rest which the soul receives from the Spirit is distinguished in several ways. It is a rest from guilt and condemnation, because we are forgiven of our sins through the blood of Jesus. It is true rest in the soul, which must not be confused with physical rest. There is nowhere promised in Scripture that we will receive rest in this life from sickness, disability, weariness, nor age. But there is a promised rest in the midst of these. It is a rest that brings us peace.

Rest that is brought by the *sanctification of the Spirit* contains specific elements. They are: rest from sin, rest from fear, rest from darkness, and rest from doubt.

1. REST FROM SIN

Sin is twofold. It is an act and it is a principle. As an act, it incurs guilt and bondage; as a principle, it incurs defilement. When sin as an act is pardoned, or forgiven, there comes rest to the soul of the sinner from the burden of guilt and bondage of sin. Therefore, the weight of condemnation and the sense of having displeased God have been removed and we have peace. But, even when the guilt of sin as an act has been pardoned, still the burden of sin as a state of heart and a tendency toward wrong doing remains entailing a sense of defilement and impurity. Even the sanctified heart still prays in earnest such as the words from this old hymn express:

> *Break off the yoke of inbred sin,*
> *And set my spirit fully free;*
> *I cannot rest till pure within,*
> *Till I am wholly lost in Thee.*

There is rest in the *sanctification of the Spirit,* which is a rest from the burden of the indwelling of sin. The Holy Spirit in its fullness enters the soul and destroys the body of sin. It crucifies it, annihilates it –kills it stone dead.

2. REST FROM FEAR

Rest from fear is not a rest from the instinctive fear of harm, sickness, or death; nor of natural timidity, but a rest from servile fear. That is, the fear of living in dread of God's commandments, God's will, and God's providences. There are many Christians who serve God under the idea that they "must". They must perform duties, they must bear crosses, they must render their services or they fear if they do not God will punish them. Hence, the duty is a task, the yoke is hard, and the burden is heavy because they are bound by fear of God's wrath. But when one is *sanctified* with the Spirit that fear is cast out, then duty is delight, service is joy, and toil is ease.

3. REST FROM DARKNESS

Rest from darkness is not rest from sorrow, disappointment, or bereavement. Nor, is it rest from evil darkness, because even though we may be *sanctified* in the Spirit and do not have darkness of condemnation, the black wing of evil sometimes spreads its presence over us and we are forced to walk in its shadow. Rest from darkness is a rest from the inward darkness present in the absence of the Holy Spirit. One may walk in the darkness of sorrow, bereavement, or temptation, yet still walk in the light of His countenance. That light is powerful enough to illuminate even the earthly midnights of trial and temptation. In this rest from darkness the sun never goes down.

4. REST FROM DOUBT

Rest from doubt is a rest from uncertainties, wonderings, and questioning. In this rest the soul takes on bold, strong opinions of assurance, knowledge, and faith in its fullness.

The rest that a person finds in the *sanctification of the Spirit* is rest from sin, from fear, from darkness, and from doubt. The Holy Spirit is the guide into this Canaan of rest. The author of this old hymn poignantly writes about the search for this rest by *the sanctification of the Spirit*. The words read like this:

> *I can see far down this mountain,*
> *Where I wandered weary years,*
> *Often hindered in my journey*
> *By the ghost of doubts and fears*
> *Broken vows and disappointments*
> *Thickly sprinkled all the way,*
> *But the Spirit led unerring*
> *To the land I hold today.*

THINK ABOUT IT...

1. *Explain your understanding of sin as an act and sin as a principle?*

2. *Do you live in fear of God?*

3. *Do you serve God because you think you "must"?*

4. *How is it possible to face sorrow, bereavement, and temptation and still have rest?*

Chapter 5

THE ADVANTAGES

REST THAT COMES with *the sanctification of the Spirit* is a *promised* rest. There is a pledge of certainty that rest is attainable and it is reality in experience. Additionally, it is a *needed* rest. The absence of this rest is a calamity and a great misfortune to the Christian character and life. Many Christians, under misapprehension, feel this rest is certainly a privilege, but not a necessity. I beg to differ. We are not delineating simply some halcyon realms of grace or some Elysian fields of spiritual blessedness whose borders are desirable, but not essential. By no means! While this rest is delightful and full of comfort, it is so much more. It is the ballast to steady our lives. It gives equilibrium to our spirit. It imparts symmetry to our Christian character. It is the indispensable reinforcement which empowers spiritual activity. The advantages of this rest are obvious.

Rest that comes with *the sanctification of the Spirit* relieves us of the weight of interior sin and weakness, so that the soul's strength goes entirely to support life's burdens of sorrow, care, and trial. Without this rest the soul breaks down into discouragement and disheartenment under the strain of its inner burdens which in turn compounds its outer burdens.

The burdens in the soul that reside in us because of the absences of *the Spirit*, induce friction with our Christian service. It is rather a vicious circle. Many Christians throw themselves into Christian service seeking relief from their inward burdens. But, in this service they find little comfort, as well as little success, because of the enfeebled and oppressed burden on their soul which consumes the strength that would otherwise make work a joy and service a delight. In other words, you cannot help others until you first help yourself; make sure your own house is in order; and, in case of an emergency an oxygen mask will drop, place it over your own mouth and nose first before attempting to assist others!

A soul that is at rest has a certain distinct manner. There is a quietness of spirit and an evenness of demeanor amidst the tempest of care, the surges of sorrow, and the tumults of our business affairs. This distinct manner impresses people with the power of grace, as nothing else can. In this world of unrest, agitation, and disquietude, a soul at rest is a spectacle so convincing it is irresistible!

I have a friend, who in her thirties, was told she had cancer. She had three small children, one of which is handicapped and required many therapy sessions and needed much help. She entered into treatments of chemotherapy and radiation. Her body was physically drained, but it always astonished me how cheerful, peaceful, and happy she was –even the days when she could not get out of bed. When you asked her, "How can you be so serene?" She would answer, "The Lord is so good. Everything will be alright!"

Don't you want what she's got?! Her tone of voice and manner of being, taught me of my need for God. Rest in the soul is power, because those who reflect the Light, help others to see it.

A soul that is at rest sets the heart, brain, nerves, hands, feet, and every power of the being toward God. It is the secret to perpetual motion in grace and constancy of peace. However, inasmuch, rest does not mean ease. Those who are most at ease have the least rest. Those who are most at rest are the least at ease. In fact, those who are most at rest have so little ease that they are troublesome to those who are at ease. People who have a soul that is at rest are so full of life that they are usually thorns in the sides of those who are looking for that rest simply by sitting in church for one hour on Sunday morning and not thinking about God for the rest of the week.

Rest that comes with *the sanctification of the Spirit* is exemplified by a soul whose ways are of pleasantness and its paths are of peace. The yoke is easy; the burden is light.

THINK ABOUT IT...

1. *What are the advantages of the rest that comes with the sanctification of the Spirit?*

2. *Do you know people who have the distinct manner of a soul at rest?*

Chapter 6

ATTAINABILITY

ONCE A PERSON has had a taste of the Spirit there comes a craving –a craving for a complete fullness of the Holy Spirit. Therefore, the soul that has come to know rest is at terrible unrest until it fully receives *the sanctification of the Spirit*. It is certainly a conundrum! But once we have recognized our need for God and turned toward Him, although we experience a rest, there is oftentimes still agitation and uneasiness because we have not yet been completely filled by *the sanctification of the Spirit*.

There is an instinctive cry of the newborn child of God as expressed in this hymn.

> *Rest for my soul I long to find,*
> *Savior, if mine Thou art,*
> *Give me Thy meek and lowly mind,*
> *And stamp Thy image on my heart.*

Even a soul that has turned to God cannot be completely satisfied until it is led by the Holy Spirit. Then the soul will sing something like these words:

> *Now rest, my long-divided heart,*
> *Fixed on this blissful center, rest.*

How do you get this rest? I hope I have made it plain to see. It is the Holy Spirit. The Holy Spirit shows us the way; not only the way *to* do it, but the way *unto* it. Whosoever will follow, will be led. It is that simple. Mere theory is a will-o'-the-wisp; mere theology is a blind gate. Neither of those can bring a soul to rest. You cannot think yourself into this rest, you cannot reason yourself into this rest, and you cannot contemplate yourself into this rest. The best human instruction available can only introduce the soul to this rest. For this very reason I cringe when I hear some evangelists say, "We must make it our life's work to save as many souls as possible!" Are you kidding me? Do these people really believe that they have been empowered to save souls? By the same token, I respond like I have heard someone scratching their fingernails down a chalkboard when I hear someone say, "God wants you to do this or that." How do they know? Anyone who tells you that they know what God is thinking, needs to be forgiven and not followed!

When a soul has come into the light of the Spirit, three things will become visible. The first is that rest in the soul is immediately accessible. The way to this rest is open to all. There is no secret code, no hidden password. There is no test of knowledge, no waiting period. There is nothing to do but to have a desiring heart. In Hebrews 4:11, Paul says, "Let us be diligent to enter that rest." The word "diligent" has the sense of "hasten." The pathway into this rest of the soul is easy. The labor of entering is not in making a way, but in hastening to travel the way that was already made for us. Once a soul has decided to enter into this rest, it may go quickly. The waters are parted, the ground is dry, and the journey is short. Many people have made this journey hard for themselves because they try to pass into this rest by their own way. All things are ready. Go.

The second is that rest in the soul is of faith. Rest and trust are inseparable. When the soul is out of a state of rest, then the soul is out of a state of trust; and when the soul is out of a state of trust, then it is out of a state of rest. Rest in the soul comes by believing. It is not reached by growth or development. Do not misunderstand; growth and development certainly have a place of importance. Growth and development bring us *to* rest, but it is faith that brings us *into* it.

Neither does the soul drift into rest. Rest does not come as a matter of course. There is a delusion to the phrase, "God, in His own good time, will give it to me." I suppose He will. But, I believe that "good time" of His is when the soul believes, not as it listlessly waits for some unknown and involuntary event to occur which may impart this rest.

Another misconception is that this rest is wages earned for hard work. It is not. You cannot "earn" your way into this rest. It is not a reward. It is a gift. The gift is there and it is ours for the taking. Notice, we must take it, which requires action on our part. Faith is the opened hand that grasps the gift of rest. Faith believes in the promise of the gift.

The third visibility of rest is that rest is in Jesus. In the Gospel of Matthew 11:28 it says, "Come to me, all you who are weary and burdened, and I will give you rest." Jesus is our burden-bearer as well as our sin-bearer. He has asked us to throw all of our cares onto Him and He becomes rest for every soul who leans on Him for repose. But, He cannot bring rest to those who come to Him if they are not willing to leave their tired, worn, and weak hearts at His feet.

THINK ABOUT IT...

    1. How do we get rest in our soul?

Chapter 7

LIBERTY

THE HUMAN SOUL was created free. It came from the hands of God unfettered of any burdens whatsoever. However, when we fell into sin, we fell into bondage. But, we have never lost our state of nature and desire for our original freedom. We have not lost our natural instinct for that liberty.

There is, in Christ, a natural freedom that is unmistakable. It is an emancipation proclamation, which is not a social or political freedom. It is not intellectual freedom, but a spiritual freedom. It is a freedom that anybody can have regardless of their social standing. It is liberty of the soul. It is a heart emancipated from the moral disability of sin.

This liberty does not emancipate the soul from physical disabilities. However, without question, there is a significant, intimate connection between body and soul. Such an intimate connection, that the body exerts a powerful influence over the temper and feeling of the soul. When the body is sick or depressed, or when the body is overcome by heat, cold, or hunger, the soul sympathizes with the body and will experience corresponding depressions, so that the soul will have less courage, less buoyancy, and less spirit.

We live in such a fast paced world that when we come to the end of each day we are fatigued, nervous, and anxiety ridden. These states can make us feel lost and hopeless and tempt us into thinking that God has abandoned us or that we have lost our faith or peace in God, when really these feelings come from physical exhaustion and nervous strain. Do you ever go to worship with a sense of dullness and being spiritless? Do you question why the message just is not getting through to you and the choir sounds like buzzing cicadas? In today's world this is not uncommon and most often is no fault of your faith. You are probably physically exhausted!

Spiritual freedom surpasses these physical disabilities. But take heart, a body in bondage from disabilities can coexist perfectly with spiritual liberty. However, there is another side to the coin. Spiritual liberty cannot coexist with bondage of the body due to sinful appetites and inclinations. You cannot be consumed by sin and enjoy spiritual liberty.

As well, spiritual liberty does not emancipate the soul from mental disabilities. Just because we have spiritual liberty does not mean that we will not still be victims of mistake, misconception, or misunderstanding. Spiritual liberty does not mean that we will be able to understand all mysteries, solve all problems, penetrate all providences, and plan unerringly for all future emergencies and work. It will not bring any such riddance from mental infirmities. In fact, spiritual liberty may easily coexist with mental weakness, infirmities, and disability. It is quite possible for a person to be holy and yet blunder. We can be made pure, yet still be perplexed.

Spiritual liberty does not emancipate the soul from sinful influence. Although Satan is not omnipresent, he is immanent to the human race and has access to the human soul. He understands us better than we do ourselves. He can powerfully influence the mind and heart. We cannot escape the presence of Satan. He can entice, distract, and darken the mind. There is no question that we will encounter the wiles of evil, and there is no promise that grace in any degree or spiritual emancipation shall deliver us from the fiery darts and hellish influence of the prince of darkness. Hence, it would be totally in vain for a person to think that spiritual liberty will put an end to all experiences of temptation and spiritual darkness.

Even in the face of this evil influence, we may still have spiritual liberty and have grace to withstand it. Remember, Christ did not come into this world to take away all of our pain, trials, and tribulation. He came in order to give us the strength to endure it. God, the Son, was made manifest in the flesh in order that He may destroy the works of

Satan. That is His mission; and, it was accomplished by His death on the Cross. Satan is a gigantic adversary and we are no match for him. We would be foolish to believe that we could pit our will against his will, our hand against his hand, our personality against his personality. His arm is longer than ours; his strength is greater than ours; his will is more powerful than ours. He is more than a match for us. The only means by which we have to defend ourselves against Satan is to turn him over to the One who was more than a match for him in the wilderness; to the One who could say, "Come out of him!" and Satan obeyed. The great secret of successful Christian warfare is, in every conflict with Satan, to give it over to Christ! Do not be discouraged, because these conflicts will recur again and again and again. But, every single time we can conquer Satan through Him who loves us and has given Himself for us.

Spiritual liberty exists even under the limitations of physical, mental, and sinful disabilities, but we need to remember that there is a difference between liberty from sin and relief from sin, just as liberty from illness is different from relief from illness. A person can be seriously ill with a painful ailment and go to the doctor, who can give him medications and painkillers. In time, the patient's pain may ease and his strength may return. He will probably be able to stop the medications. However, there is no certainty that the illness will not recur. He has had relief from the illness, but not liberty from it. Likewise, it is possible to have relief from sin and not have liberty from sin. Relief from sin is simply to be removed from the ache of conscience. Many people are constantly seeking a treatment for relief from sin. And when relief is all that is sought, they backslide, become worldly, lose their enjoyment of life, and lapse into wrongdoing. They feel so miserable and suffer such spiritual horrors that they turn and seek relief again. It is another vicious cycle. Indeed, for many people a great part their commitment to church is in effort to receive spiritual relief. What we ought to be seeking is spiritual restoration and liberty from sin. Where the Holy Spirit is, there is liberty from sin. It is by allowing the Holy Spirit into our hearts that we find that liberty.

THINK ABOUT IT...

1. *Do you often have a sense of dullness and being spiritless?*

2. *How do we find liberty from sin?*

3. *In your own words, describe spiritual liberty.*

Chapter 8

THE BONDAGE OF SIN

WHEN WE HARBOR sin in our hearts, we are truly in bondage. The bondage of sin consists of a threefold power: first, its existence; second, its fear; and third, its weakness. It is these forces of sin which bring us into captivity. But, from each of these there can be freedom.

1. FREEDOM FROM THE PRESENCES OF SIN

Sin is of a twofold nature. It is a voluntary transgression of the law, and it is also a state of the soul, condition of the heart, and an inclination toward evil. Phrases and words that describe this sinful state of the soul are numerous, both in Scripture and the secular world. We have all heard of at least one of these phrases: the sin that dwells in us, the carnal mind, the old man, the flesh, inbred sin, root of bitterness, remains of evil. Whatever name you call it, whatever term you use to define it, it is easily recognized as that state of heart by which it is easy to do wrong and difficult to do right. It is that which makes us inclined to be worldly and neglectful. It is that which gives us an affinity toward envy, jealousy, anger, pride, willfulness, and being uncharitable. It is the source of aversion to that which is spiritual, producing often disrelish for prayer, for reading the Bible, and for holy conversations and associations. These are only some of the manifestations of the presence of sin as a state of the soul. What a bondage this truly is –there is a promise to the soul at peace, impelling us one way and the sin that dwells within us drawing us the other.

This burden of inner conflict causes us to cry within our hearts. The words of this hymn exemplify what the heart cries:

> Rest my soul I long to find,
> Savior of all, if mine Thou art,
> Give me Thy meek and lowly mind,
> And stamp Thine image on my heart.
> Break off the yoke of inbred sin,
> And freely set my spirit free;
> I cannot rest till pure within,
> Till I am wholly lost in Thee.

Christ can emancipate us from the inbeing of sin as fully as from the guilt of sin.

> ***"As far as the east is from the west, so far has He removed our transgressions from us." (Psalms 103:12 NAS)***

> ***"For I know my transgressions, and my sin is ever before me." (Psalms 51:3 NAS)***

> ***"Wash me, and I shall be whiter than snow." (Psalms 51:7 NAS)***

Christ can make us free from sin *in* us. Which is not to be confused to include freedom from temptation to sin, but it does mean such a deliverance from the love of sin that the probabilities of resisting temptation are in favor of the soul. So long as sin is in the soul, its dip is toward evil. Hence, when the dip is toward evil, then when we are under the powerful influence of temptation it is easy to fall into sin. Think about it this way –a tree that is inclined southward easily falls to the south, but if the tree is inclined northward, it is very difficult to make it fall to the south. So too, when the soul has a tendency toward sin, it readily falls into sin, but when the tendency toward sin has been destroyed in the soul and there is a powerful inclination toward holiness, the likelihood of falling into sin is greatly reduced! That is not to say that the soul cannot yield to sin, but it does not want to yield to sin. Sin is now abhorrent to the soul and holiness is most agreeable. It is by the indwelling of Christ that the soul is delivered from the inbeing of sin. The soul now will have an impulse to resent sin and a desire to take up arms against it. While freedom from the presence of sin as a state of the soul does not emancipate us from the temptation of sin, it does impart a wonderful ability for resisting it.

2. Freedom from the Fear of Sin

It is a condition of human nature that we become victims of the things we dread. If we are fearful of being alone in the house then, when we are alone in the house we are afraid. Sin is not something that we should fear. If we do fear it, it is that much more likely that we will fall into it. It is the dread of sin that keeps so many in its fetters. Let us look at it from another direction. Have you ever known anyone who did not want to go to church or to claim himself a Christian because he feared that he would not be able to live up to its standards or feared that he would not be able to give up his sinful ways? So instead, he went back to his own cup and wallowed in the mire of dissipation. Likewise, if somebody does make the leap of faith into trusting God but begins to says, "I do not think I can really turn away from my sinful nature," the likelihood is that they will soon fall back and even into a more oppressive state than before. What are they thinking anyway when they say they do not think they can do it? Do they think that Jesus means to mock them when He says that He will be your strength and keep you? If this is what you believe then you might as well give up now. Let your faith supplant your fear!

3. Freedom from the Weakness of Sin

Sin in the soul is a morally and spiritually debilitating thing; it is like a hidden disease in the body. The most common ailment in the church today is spiritual weakness. Overall, there is a general complaint of weak faith and impotent joy. This in not just a complaint of visitors and new members; it is a complaint from ministers, class leaders, and members of longstanding. It is a humiliating confession from those to whom we look for strength when they say, "I can do nothing," or "I am powerless to help." This spiritual weakness has brought them to a point where duty to them is a load and worship to them is a task.

So what is the source of spiritual weakness? I say that it is sin in the soul. Sin in any degree which remains in your heart is a consumption devouring spiritual vigor. Sin in the heart is an impoverishing thing, a starvation process by which the soul is held in bondage.

When sin is taken out of the heart the source of spiritual debility is removed. Thus, the soul has liberty! It is free from the *presence*, the *fear*, and the *weakness* of sin. Emancipation!

At first glace, it appears that the atonement through Christ delivers us only from the *curse* of sin. But as we continue to grow spiritually we see that not only does it deliver us from the *curse* of sin, but it also delivers us from the *condemnation* of sin. And, as we continue to grow even more we see further into the depths of atonement and understand that it not only delivers us from the *curse* and *condemnation* of sin, but also from the *corruption* of sin.

The curse and condemnation of sin are the outer walls of the prison that keeps us in bondage, but it is the corruption of sin that is the inner walls of the prison. When the corruption of sin is destroyed then the inner walls of the prison are burst open and the soul is set free. Where the Spirit of the Lord is, there is liberty!

 **THINK ABOUT IT…**

1. *What are the three elements of the bondage of sin?*

2. *What are the two natures of sin?*

3. *How are we delivered from the inbeing of sin?*

4. *Are you inclined toward wrongdoing or godliness?*

5. *What is the source of spiritual weakness?*

Chapter 9

ON BECOMING A SERVANT OF GOD

THE PHRASE, "YOU cannot serve two masters," has almost become a cliché. But, cliché or not, it is a most valid phrase. Who is your master? God or sin? You cannot serve both.

> *"No one can serve two masters; for either he will hate the one and love the other, or he will hold to one and despise the other." (Matthew 6:24 NAS)*

That is why the soul must be made free from sin –the servitude to sin must be broken. When the soul ceases to be a slave to sin, it bounds into the exalted sphere of a servant to God. So-much-as we serve sin, in-so-much-as we fail to be servants of God. It is not possible to become a true servant of God so long as you are in bondage to sin in your soul.

One reason so many Christians find the way hard is because they are attempting to serve God at the same time they are serving self, sin, and the world. And, they wonder why it is so difficult to serve God. It is because they are under the wrong taskmaster. But when we make the taskmaster God, then running His errands, doing His work, and accomplishing His will becomes easy.

The greatest thing that was ever said about Moses was uttered by God to Joshua when God appointed Joshua, the successor of Moses. God said to him, "My servant Moses is dead." God did not say, "The world's best historian is dead," nor did He say, "The most wonderful law-giver is dead," or "The greatest warrior is dead," or "The most matchless leader is dead." No, God said, "My servant is dead." The Apostle Paul was also quick to call himself a servant of Christ.

When you are a servant of God, nothing, however humble, is undignified. Lowly deeds, unknown acts, the least services to the least ones, offered cups of cold water, silent prayers, unpretentious words and unbidden tears are great achievements because they are done as a servant of God, at His bidding and for His glory. And when one is a servant of God they know the compensation for all the pain, toil, and sacrifice they may incur. As a true servant of God, we no longer crave appreciation, position, or renown. We find our honor in being a servant of God alone. In a secular conception there are many tasks considered humble, undignified, and insignificant –but, when done for the Master, they are most honorable and glorious! As servants of God we are exalted to the position of high ministers, royal ambassadors, Heaven's agents, and Heaven's heirs. Whatever our condition by earthly means may be, even to the depths of poverty, chains, sorrow, or obscurity –nothing can deprive us of our high honor of being a servant to God. It is a blessed thing to be a servant of God!

> *"No longer will there be any curse. The throne of God and of the Lamb will be in the city, and His servants will serve Him. They will see His face, and His name will be on their foreheads." (Revelation 22:3-4)*

Holiness is a most wonderful quality of the Christian experience. Being made free from sin is the emptying of the soul by the purging power of the Holy Spirit through the blood. Holiness is the filling, transforming, sanctifying power of the Holy Spirit. It imparts to the soul all the mind of Christ, and all the fullness of God. But, to become holy we must first be cleansed and made free from sin. Holiness immediately succeeds cleansing. The glorious experience of holiness is the immediate result of spiritual freedom from sin.

THINK ABOUT IT...

1. *Who is your master?*

2. *Do you find it difficult to serve God?*

3. *Do you desire recognition for the work you do for God?*

4. *In your own words describe what it means to be holy?*

Chapter 10

REASONABLE BELIEVING

EVERYTHING WHICH WE have discussed relies on evidence which is beyond the scope of human understanding, therefore, making it difficult for many to believe. But, any evidence that was in the scope of human understanding would not be sufficient. If that were the case, then we would be using our frames of mind, our feelings and emotions, our conceptions of the imagination, and our determination of will as a basis of faith. It would not be believing in God, it would be believing in ourselves. If you say you cannot believe, then here is the question that you need to ask, "Whom is it that you cannot believe?" Most likely you are referring to yourself, and my response is, "Thank goodness! That is one person you do not have to believe!"

> *"Now faith is being sure of what we hope for and certain of what we do not see." (Hebrews 11:1)*

The above Scripture is not a definition of faith; it is a delineation of faith. It is believing as a principle or activity of the human soul. It describes the very nature of faith. Hence, faith becomes the equivalent of things hoped for, and the demonstration of things not seen. It is the gracious element of believing. Jesus said, "All things are possible to him who believes." The effects of faith are supernatural, because faith itself is supernatural. Faith constitutes a supernatural believing. However, faith is not a spiritual entity, ready-made, which God just drops into the hearts of people for the purpose of believing. It is by the operation of the Holy Spirit when the human soul begins seeking, looking, and asking.

We have been given a supernatural basis for believing. It is Scripture.

> *"For everything that was written in the past was written to teach us, so that through endurance and the encouragement of the Scriptures we might have hope." (Romans 15:4)*

As the eye responds to light, and the ear to sound, so does the soul to the truth of God's Word. Every soul has been given the ability to believe. Potentially, all people are believers. "Thomas the doubter" is a misnomer. Faith is natural; unbelief is unnatural. Doubt is willful; unbelief is carnal. The sin of unbelief is that we can believe, but will not believe. Why is it that when we have the ability to believe that we, the poor conscience-smitten soul, contrite, struggling to find peace and rest, would not look up and do the supernatural thing of believing. This is unnatural!

THINK ABOUT IT...

    1. What is faith?

    2. Do you have faith?

A FINAL THOUGHT…

1. *Before you read this book, had you ever heard the word sanctification? Did you know the definition of sanctification?*

2. *What is your understanding of sanctification?*

3. *How has this book enabled you to seek a deeper relationship with God?*

NOTES

Pamela Jackson

NOTES

NOTES

www.ingramcontent.com/pod-product-compliance
Lightning Source LLC
Chambersburg PA
CBHW031428040426
42444CB00006B/729